D0953065

# Little Book...

# Big Thoughts

James M. Lawson

© James M. Lawson 1963

Library of Congress Catalog Card Number A 673348

Second Printing

*Printed in the United States of America*

WITTMAN PRINTING COMPANY

556 Clay Street • San Francisco, California

"We" who have brought these sayings to you are an innumerable people. From thousands of years in time and numberless miles of space these quotations have marched up to the door of your thought.

Quotations have enriched my life with much encouragement, inspiration, pleasure and deep satisfaction. From various sources these attractive sayings have come to my attention and caused this collection to grow with the years.

When rereading some of these pertinent gems of thought there was a repeating of "Someday I should make a scrapbook of these."

It is interesting that a quotation was the deciding force which impelled me to do something about it. . . . "The wisdom of the wise and the experiences of the ages are perpetuated by quotation."

—*Benjamin Disraeli*

With grateful appreciation to family, friends, Benjamin Disraeli, and all who have in any way contributed, these good sayings are brought to you.

This is the story of "Little book — Big Thoughts." May these selections be as helpful to you as they are to me and even more so.

Sincerely yours,

*James M. Lawson*

The way to love God is to love many things.

—*Vincent Van Gough*

From his cradle to his grave a man never does a single thing which has any first and foremost object save one—to secure peace of mind, spiritual comfort, for himself.

—*Mark Twain*

We live in deeds, not years; in thoughts, not breaths.

—*P. J. Bailey*

The charm of a deed is its doing; the charm of life is its living; the soul of the thing is the thought.

—*Eugene Fitch Ware*

What lies behind us and what lies before us are tiny matters compared with what lies within us.

—*William Worrow*

A period of high civilization is one in which thoughts fly freely from mind to mind, from one country to another — yes, from the past into the present.

—*Gilbert Highet*

You must give some time to your fellowman. Even if it's a little thing, do something for those who have need of help, something for which you get no pay but the privilege of doing it. For remember, you don't live in a world all your own. Your brothers are here too.

—*Albert Schweitzer*

Whether a man lives or dies in vain can be measured only by the way he faces his problems, both the success or failure of the inner conflict within his own soul. And of this no one knows save God.

—*James Conant*

He who resents his problems becomes their victim.

—*JML*

Those who can but don't, must give way to those who try.

—*JML*

Much of the truth is found upon the battlefields of controversy and is kept alive by sharp exchanges.

—*Lawrence A. Kipton*

Nature has made two sorts of excellent intellects: one kind to produce beautiful thoughts or actions; the other to admire them.

—*Joseph Joubert*

Religion . . . is the forerunner of international law because it alone can create the international spirit, the international obligation.

—*William Ernest Hocking*

Every thought which genius and piety throw into the world alters the world.

—*Ralph Waldo Emerson*

A bird lighting on a rock makes some impression.

—*John Muir*

The mind ought sometimes to be amused that it may better return to thought and itself.

—*Phaedrus*

There is nothing either good or bad but thinking makes it so.

—*Shakespeare*

All things that we see standing accomplished in the world are properly the outer material result, the practical realization, and embodiment of thoughts that dwell in the great men sent into the world.

—*Carlyle*

Real knowledge, like everything else of the highest value, is not obtained easily. It must be worked for, studied for, and thought for; and more than all, it must be prayed for.

—*Thomas Arnold*

The light comes as we work toward it.

—*Jacob A. Riis*

Someday the scientists will turn their laboratories over to the study of God and prayer, and the spiritual forces which as yet have hardly been scratched.

*—Charles P. Steinmetz*

Angels. God's thoughts passing to man; spiritual intuitions, pure and perfect; the inspiration of goodness, purity, and immortality, counteracting all evil, sensuality, and mortality.

*—Mary Baker Eddy*

Man's work is to labor and leaven — as best he may — earth here with heaven.

*—Robert Browning*

For as he thinketh in his heart, so is he.

*—Proverbs*

Nurture your mind with great thoughts, for to believe in the heroic makes heroes.

*—Beaconsfield*

Great minds discuss ideas, average minds discuss events, shallow minds discuss people.

*—Anon.*

The way of the superior man is threefold: Virtuous, he is free from anxieties; Wise, he is free from perplexities; Bold, he is free from fear.

*—Confucius*

A free life is the only life worthy of a human being. That which is not free is not responsible, and that which is not responsible is not moral. In other words, freedom is a condition of morality.

—*Thomas Davidson*

There is only one thing that will really train the human mind and that is the voluntary use of the mind by the man himself. You may aid him, you may guide him, you may suggest to him, and above all, you may inspire him. But the only thing worth having is that which he gets by his own exertion, which he gets in direct proportion to what he puts into it.

—*A. L. Lowell*

Men buy success by giving up a host of things they want for what they want most.

—*Arthur Guiterman*

It is more important to know where you are going than to get there quickly. Do not mistake activity for achievement.

—*Mabel Newcomber*

Grasp an idea and work it out to a successful conclusion. That is about all there is in life for any of us.

—*Edward Harriman*

The highest possible stage in moral culture is when we recognize that we ought to control our thoughts.

—*Charles R. Darwin*

Life affords no higher pleasure than that of surmounting difficulties, passing from one step of success to another, forming new wishes and seeing them gratified. He that labors in any great or laudable undertaking has his fatigues first supported by hope and afterwards rewarded by joy.

*—Samuel Johnson*

The vision of the ideal guards the monotony of work from becoming the monotony of life.

*—Westcott*

He is a man of sense who does not grieve for what he has not, but rejoices in what he has.

*—Epictetus*

When a man realizes his littleness, his greatness can appear.

*—H.G. Wells*

Truth travels down from the heights of philosophy to the humblest walks of life, and up from the simplest perceptions of an awakened intellect to the discoveries which almost change the face of the world. At every stage of its progress it is genial, luminous, creative.

*—Edward Everett*

Age should not have its face lifted but rather teach the world to admire wrinkles as the etchings of experience and the firm lines of character.

*—Ralph Barton Perry*

No wise man ever wishes to be younger.

*—Anon.*

A talent can be cultivated in tranquility; character, only in the rushing stream of life.

*—Goethe*

All the problems of the world could be settled easily if men were only willing to think.

*—Dr. Nicholas Murray Butler*

Men exist for the sake of one another. Teach them then or bear with them.

*—Marcus Aurelius*

The ability to think straight, some knowledge of the past, some vision of the future, some skill to do useful service, some urge to fit that service into the well-being of the community — these are the most vital things education must try to produce.

*—Virginia C. Gildersleeve*

Teach the young people how to think, not what to think.

*—Sidney Sugarman*

The true test of a university's success is not the discoveries and inventions which its professors make or the books they write, but the sort of people its students turn out to be.

*—Clarence Tracy*

The best teacher is . . . the one who kindles an inner fire, arouses moral enthusiasm, inspires the student with a vision of what he may become and reveals the worth and permanency of moral and spiritual and cultural values.

—*Harold Garnet*

It is not given to any man, however endowed, to rise spontaneously into intellectual splendor without the parentage of antecedent thought.

—*John Tyndall*

Wisdom comes not from experience but from meditating on experience and assimilating it.

—*Joy Elmer Morgan*

The best teacher is willing to be forgotten. His only reassurance needs to be the faith that somehow his efforts have increased the amount of mind in a world which can never have too much of that commodity. His final reward is the quality of his life, which teaching has helped to shape.

—*Mark Van Doren*

Teachers open the door — you enter by yourself.

—*Anon.*

To him whose elastic and vigorous thought keeps pace with the sun, the day is a perpetual morning.

—*Thoreau*

You can't stop people from thinking, but you can start them.

—*Frank A. Dusch*

Power is built up only to fall unless it rests on the one solid basis — the basis of Spirit. The continual struggle to preserve the moral basis of the nation's strength — through the arts, education and thought — is the strongest bulwark of national security.

—*Jaime Torres Bodet*

The love of liberty is the love of others; the love of power is the love of ourselves.

—*William Hazlitt*

The true purpose of education is to cherish and unfold the seed of immortality already sown within us; to develop, to their fullest extent, the capacities of every kind with which the God who made us has endowed us.

—*Anna Jameson*

The one Mind, God, contains no mortal opinions. All that is real is included in this immortal Mind.

—*Mary Baker Eddy*

What is done in the classrooms today will be reflected in the successes or failures of civilization tomorrow.

—*Lindy C. Baxter*

Education is leading human souls to what is best, and making what is best out of them; and these two objects are always attainable together, and by the same means. The training which makes men happiest in themselves makes them most serviceable to others.

—*John Ruskin*

Greater than even the greatest discovery is to keep open the way to future discovery.

—*John Jacob Abel*

Questioning is like standing at a gate and reaching to raise the latch. It is a sign that one has reached a state of development where an awareness of truth prompts the interrogation. Nothing can or ever will be forced through to one who has not lifted the latch of receptivity. Live each day alerted to the realization that voices speak to ears that listen.

—*Joseph H. Brooks*

Good deeds are trophies erected in the hearts of men.

—*Zenophon*

Learn as if you were to live forever; live as if you were to die tomorrow.

—*Anon.*

Different sects, like different clocks, may be all near the matter, although they don't quite agree.

—*Anon.*

The best sermon ever preached is Truth practised and demonstrated by the destruction of sin, sickness, and death.

—*Mary Baker Eddy*

The miracles of the Church seem to me to rest not so much upon faces or voices or healing power coming suddenly near to us from afar off, as upon our perceptions being made finer, so that for a moment our eyes can see and our ears can hear what is there about us always.

—*Willa Cather*

Our ideal will never be met in life unless we have first achieved it within ourselves.

—*Maeterlinck*

Why go outside when all is within?

—*Chinese Proverb*

The kingdom of God is within you.

—*Christ Jesus*

He who will not reason is a bigot; he who cannot is a fool; and he who dares not is a slave.

—*Henry Drummond*

It is man's mission to learn to understand.

—*Vannevar Bush*

Knowledge comes by taking things apart—analysis. But wisdom comes by putting things together.

*—John A. Morrison*

Everything great or good is ours if we have the humility to accept it.

*—Vinson*

Tension cannot long remain where Love's healing power is flowing freely.

*—JML*

It is better not to live than not to love.

*—Henry Drummond*

All the law is fulfilled in one word, even this: Thou shalt love thy neighbor as thyself.

*—Galatians*

Faults are thick where love is thin.

*—Anon.*

As ye would that men should do unto you, do ye also to them likewise.

*—Christ Jesus*

Every blade of grass has its share of the dews of heaven.

*—Anon.*

There is neither Jew nor Greek, there is neither bond nor free, there is neither male nor female, for ye are all one in Christ Jesus.

—*Galatians*

Like the star that shines afar,
Without haste, and without rest;
Let each man wheel with steady sway
Round the task that rules today,
And do his best.

—*Goethe*

Better suffer a great evil than do a little one.

—*Anon.*

The rewards of duty are not rest from labor, but greater tasks.

—*Follen*

Sin is not hurtful because it is forbidden, but it is forbidden because it is hurtful.

—*Anon.*

A gem is not polished without rubbing, nor a man perfected without trials.

—*Chinese Proverb*

Anger is often more hurtful than the injury that caused it.

—*Anon.*

A man who has committed a mistake and does not correct it is committing another mistake.

*—Confucius*

What is the use of running when we are not on the right road?

*—Anon.*

A house without books is like a room without windows.

*—Horace Mann*

Except a living man, there is nothing more wonderful than a book; a message to us from the dead — human souls we never saw, who lived perhaps thousands of miles away. And yet these, in those little sheets of paper, speak to us, arouse us, . . . teach us, comfort us, open their hearts to us as brothers.

*—Charles Kingsley*

The Bible is a book of faith, and a book of doctrine, and a book of morals, and a book of religion. But it is also a book which teaches man his own responsibility, his own dignity and equality with his fellow man.

*—Daniel Webster*

Books are the quietest and most constant of friends; they are the most accessible and wisest of counsellors and the most patient of teachers.

*—Charles W. Eliot*

The books which help you most are those which make you think the most. The hardest way of learning is by easy reading. But a great book that comes from a great thinker — is a ship of thought, deep-freighted with truth and beauty.

*—Theodore Parker*

A book introduces new thoughts, but it cannot make them speedily understood. It is the task of the sturdy pioneer to hew the tall oak and to cut the rough granite. Future ages must declare what the pioneer has acomplished.

*—Mary Baker Eddy*

If we are to become masters of science, not its slaves, we must learn to use its immense power to good purpose. The machine itself has neither mind nor soul nor moral sense. Only man has been endowed with these Godlike attributes. Every age has its destined duty. Ours is to nurture an awareness of those divine attributes and a sense of responsibility in giving them expression.

*—David Sarnoff*

Truth is the discipline of the ascetic, the quest of the mystic, the faith of the simple, the ransom of the weak, the standard of the righteous, the doctrine of the meek, and the challenge of Nature. Together, all these constitute the Law of the Universe.

*—John Hay Allison*

If a man does not keep pace with his companions, perhaps he hears a different drummer.

*—Henry David Thoreau*

The egg's no chick by falling from the hen, nor man a Christian till he's born again.

—*John Bunyan*

Truth is a thing immortal and perpetual, and it gives to us a beauty that fades not away in time, nor does it take away the freedom of speech which proceeds from justice; but it gives to us the knowledge of what is just and lawful, separating from the unjust and refuting them.

—*Epictetus*

Speech is a pump and pours out the water from the great lake of Thought — whither it flows back again.

—*John Sterling*

The time for thinkers has come.

—*Mary Baker Eddy*

You cannot travel within and stand still without.

—*James Allen*

The stumbling block becomes the stepping stone when wisely used.

—*JML*

The sages do not consider that making no mistake is a blessing. They believe, rather, that the great virtue of a man lies in his ability to correct his mistakes and continually make a new man of himself.

—*Wang Yang-Ming*

The wise man is informed in what is right, the inferior man in what will pay.

—*Confucius*

The heart carries the feet.

—*Simeon Ashkemazi*

No one who really has knowledge fails to practice it. Knowledge without practice should be interpreted as lack of knowledge.

—*Wang Yang-Ming*

Wisdom is ofttimes nearer when we stoop than when we soar.

—*Wordsworth*

God is the great house that holds all His children, and we dwell in Him as the fish dwell in the sea.

—*Anon.*

Who lives in good, lives also in God, — lives in all Life, through all space.

—*Mary Baker Eddy*

Human felicity is produced not so much by great pieces of good fortune that seldom happen, as by little advantages that occur every day.

*—Benjamin Franklin*

Most people would succeed in small things if they were not troubled by great ambitions.

*—Henry Wadsworth Longfellow*

Trifles make perfection, but perfection is no trifle.

*—Anon.*

Ideals are like stars; you will not succeed in touching them with your hands. But like the seafaring man on the desert of waters, you choose them as your guides, and, following them, you will reach your destiny.

*—Carl Schurz*

Faith ends where worry begins, and worry ends where faith begins.

*—George Muller*

Peace cannot be kept by force: it can be achieved only by understanding.

*—Albert Einstein*

The spice of life is battle; the friendliest relations are still a kind of contest.

—*Robert Louis Stevenson*

Friendship is the allay of our sorrows, the ease of our passions, the discharge of our oppressions, the sanctuary to our calamities, the counsellor of our doubts, the clarity of our minds, the emission of our thoughts, the exercise and improvement of what we dedicate.

—*Edward Everett*

Greater love hath no man than this, that a man lay down his life for his friends.

—*Christ Jesus*

Hast thou a friend, and forgettest to be grateful?

—*Mary Baker Eddy*

If you must tell me your opinions, tell me what you believe in. I have plenty of doubts of my own.

—*Goethe*

The only way in which one human being can properly attempt to influence another is to encourage him to think for himself.

—*Leslie Stephen*

If you would have a friend — be one.

—*Anon.*

The highest value of work is not what you get for it, but what you become by it.

—*John Ruskin*

Music means more to me the longer I live. I cannot imagine what it will be like when I am an hundred.

—*Bruno Walter*

Music demands of us men and women that we attain a composure, an inwardness that will enable us to raise to life something of the deep spirit that lies within it.

—*Albert Schweitzer*

If I had my life to live over again, I would have made a rule to read some poetry and listen to some music at least once a week; for perhaps the parts of my brain now atrophied would have thus kept active through use. The loss of these tastes is the loss of happiness and may possibly be injurious to the intellect by enfeebling the emotional part of our nature.

—*Charles Darwin*

Past experience should be a guide post, not a hitching post.

—*D. W. Williams*

If you pursue good with labor, the labor passes away, but the good remains; if you pursue evil with pleasure, the pleasure passes away, but the evil remains.

—*Anon.*

It should be our purpose in life to see that each of us make such contributions as will enable us to say that we, individually and collectively, are a part of the answer to the world problem and not a part of the problem itself.

—*Andrew Cordier*

Sensual pleasures are ours for the taking, no down payment required. Heavy payments must be made thereafter as long as these selfish pleasures are kept. Spiritual pleasures must be earned and paid for in advance. These are ours forever.

—*JML*

Your disposition will be suitable to that which you most frequently think on, for the soul is, as it were, tinged with the color and complexion of its own thoughts.

—*Marcus Antonius*

How precious also are thy thoughts unto me, Oh God! How great is the sum of them!

—*Psalms*

God gave every man individuality of constitution and a chance of achieving individuality of character. He puts special instruments into every man's hands by which to make himself and achieve his mission.

—*J. G. Holland*

The most fertile soil does not necessarily produce the most abundant harvest. It is the use we make of our faculties which renders them valuable.

—*T. W. Higginson*

Whatever may be the means, or whatever the more immediate end of any kind of art, all of it that is good agrees in this, that it is the expression of one soul talking to another and is precious according to the greatness of the soul that utters it.

*—John Ruskin*


There is no contingency whatever but we may draw from it that perpetual growth of inward strength which, when all is said, is the one and only secret of what is called happiness.

*—J. L. Garvin*


Most people don't recognize opportunity because he's wearing work clothes.

*—Henry Kaiser*


Wealth is not his that has it, but his that enjoys it.

*—Anon.*


Money is a good servant but a dangerous master.

*—Anon.*


Wisdom is a good purchase, though we pay dearly for it.

*—Anon.*


First deserve, then desire.

*—Anon.*


Nothing is enough for the man to whom enough is too little.

*—Epicurus*

Great bashfulness is oftener the effect of pride than modesty.

—*Lord Halifax*

Success is not what our ancestors have built, but what we can build by our own effort to be governed by moral law, the law of God.

—*JML*

Nothing is worth more than this day.

—*Goethe*

Failure is more often frequently from want of energy than from want of capital.

—*Daniel Webster*

Nothing resembles pride as much as discouragement.

—*Amiel*

The man who commands efficiently must have obeyed others in the past.

—*Cicero*

Before you run in double harness, look well to the other horse.

—*Anon.*

Don't burn up your blanket to get rid of a flea.

—*Turkish Prov.*

Fleas have other fleas to bite 'em, and these have their fleas ad infinitum.

—*Anon.*

Our mistakes won't irreparably damage our lives unless we let them. It is said that in making Persian rugs the artist stands before the rug while a group of boys stand behind to pull the thread after the artist starts it. If one of the boys makes a mistake, the artist adjusts the pattern accordingly so that when the rug is finished no one can tell where the mistake was made. The same kind of adjustment will take place in our lives if we but let go of the mental thread of each mistake and let God weave it into a successful, orderly pattern.

—*James E. Sweaney*

It is by patience and self control that the truly heroic character is perfected.

—*Samuel Smiles*

The morality of an action depends upon the motive from which we act.

—*Samuel Johnson*

You can bear your own faults, why not a fault of your wife?

—*Anon.*

The only failure a man ought to fear is failure to cleave to the purpose he sees to be best.

—*George Eliot*

In all living there is a certain narrowness of application which leads to breadth of power. We have to concentrate on a thing in order to master it. Then we must be broad enough not to be narrowed by our specialties.

—*Rev. Ralph W. Sockman*

Every now and then go away, have a little relaxation, for when you come back to your work your judgment will be surer; since to remain constantly at work will cause you to lose power of judgment . . . Go some distance away because then the work appears smaller, and more of it can be taken in at a glance, and a lack of harmony or proportion is more readily seen.

—*Leonardo da Vinci*

It is a thin board that does not have two sides.

—*Texas Proverb*

To live, mankind must recover its essential humaneness and its innate divinity; men must recover their capacity for humility, sanity and integrity; soldiers and civilians must see their hope in some other world than one completely dominated by the physical and chemical sciences.

—*George F. G. Stanley*

Pure gold does not fear the smelter.

—*Chinese Proverb*

Alcoholism and race consciousness are two conspicuous sources of danger to western civilization. A mixture of atheism, materialism, socialism, and alcoholism has been the cause of the decline and decay of 19 out of 21 civilizations.

—*Arnold Toynbee*

Drink does not drown care, but waters it and makes it grow faster.

—*Anon.*

Dear God and Father of us all, forgive our foolish ways.

—*John Greenleaf Whittier*


In looking back over our lives, we often see that what seemed at the time the worst hours and the most hopeless . . . were in reality the best of all. They developed powers within us that had heretofore slept, developed energies of which we had never dreamed.

—*James Freeman Clark*


The birds are moulting. If man could only moult also — his mind, once a year its errors; his heart, once a year its useless passions!

—*T. L. Allen*


Liberty is the one thing you cannot have unless you give it to others.

—*Walter A. White*


They are slaves who fear to speak for the fallen and the weak. They are slaves who dare not be in the right with two or three.

—*James Russell Lowell*


The only difference between a rut and a grave is their dimensions.

—*Ellen Glasgow*


Love, redolent with unselfishness, bathes all in beauty and light

—*Mary Baker Eddy*

Love rules the court, the camp, the grove; for love is heaven, and heaven is love.

—*Sir Walter Scott*

Put a match to the fuel and the flame will appear; turn your heart to divine Love and God's blessings will appear.

—*JML*

A soft answer turneth away wrath.

—*Proverbs*

Fill your heart with absolute goodness and all evil disappears.

—*JML*

No longer talk at all about the kind of man that a good man ought to be, but be such.

—*Marcus Aurelius*

Create in me a clean heart O God, and renew a right spirit within me.

—*Psalms of David*

Only let me make my life simple and straight, like a flute of reed, for Thee to fill with music.

—*Rabindranath Tagore*

Those who succeed alone with Love may then enjoy success together.

—*JML*

There is no fear in love, but perfect love casteth out fear:
And this commandment have we from him, That he who loveth
God love his brother also.
He that loveth not knoweth not God; for God is love.

—*I John*

Love is not one of the attributes of God, but the sum of them all.

—

If you do what you should not, you must bear what you would
not.

Jesus never gave cause for the belief that even his own sacrifice
on the cross could by any process of mental gymnastics serve
as a substitute for man's fulfillment of his obligation to society.

—*Carl Wallace Miller*

Render therefore unto Caesar the things which are Caesar's;
and unto God the things that are God's.

—*Christ Jesus*

Refuse the testimony of material sense and gain the sense of
life in God, Spirit.

—*JML*

Your daily life is your temple and your religion.

—*Kahlil Gibran*

God supports only our uprightness for He is equally near in all
directions.

—*JML*

A heart in love with beauty never grows old.

Charity is the key to heaven.

Every Pharoah has his Moses.

You can't make a stallion of a donkey by clipping his ears.

A red apple invites stones.

—*Turkish Proverbs*

Is there a greater enemy than anger, which kills both laughter and joy? Chain anger, lest it chain thee.

—*Cura Hindu*

Am I perpetuating a problem or living the right answer?

—*JML*

There is no deception quite so great or so dangerous as self-deception.

—*William Parker*

No one has a right to add to the sorrows of the world by shedding gloom around. Every person creates a certain soul atmosphere, and from his personality radiates whatever of light he has to give.

—*Henry Ward Beecher*

The highest wisdom and the highest genius have been invariably accompanied with cheerfulness. We have sufficient proofs on record that Shakespeare and Socrates were the most festive companions.

*—Thomas Love Peacock*

A cheerful friend is like a sunny day, shedding brightness on all around.

*—Sir John Lubbock*

Resolve to be happy, your joy and you shall form an invincible host against difficulties.

*—Helen Keller*

God loveth a cheerful giver.

*—II Corinthians*

Your joy can no man take from you.

*—Christ Jesus*

Happy is the man that findeth wisdom and the man that getteth understanding.

*—Proverbs*

Good sayings are like pearls strung together.

*—Anon.*

Every man must live with the man he makes of himself.

*—JML*

The only way to get rid of responsibilities is to discharge them.

—*Walter S. Robertson*

I know that the man who shows me his wealth is like the beggar who shows me his poverty: they are both asking alms of me.

—*Ben Hecht*

Giving is living.

—*Anon.*

The wise men of antiquity when they wished to make the whole world peaceful and happy first put their own states into proper order. Before putting their states into proper order, they regulated their families; before regulating their families, they regulated themselves. Before regulating themselves they tried to be sincere in their thoughts, and before being sincere in their thoughts, they tried to see things exactly as they really were.

—*Confucius*

I am ready to allow that the ultimate cause of all motion is immaterial — that is God.

—*Charles Darwin*

In character, in manners, in style, in all things, the supreme excellence is simplicity.

—*Longfellow*

What I ought to do, I can, and if I can, I surely must.

—*C. W. Hetzler*

You will find poetry nowhere, unless you bring some with you.

—*Joseph Joubert*

Writing or printing is like shooting with a rifle: you may hit your reader's mind or miss it. But talking is like playing at a mark with the pipe of an engine; if it is within reach, and you have time enough, you can't help hitting it.

—*Oliver W. Holmes*

But hushed be every thought that springs from the bitterness of things.

—*Wordsworth*

To endure is greater than to dare; to tire out hostile fortune; to be daunted by no difficulty; to keep heart when all have lost it; to go through intrigue spotless;—who can say this is not greatness?

—*William Makepeace Thackeray*

Nothing truly can be termed my own but that which I make my own by using well; those deeds of charity which we have done shall stay forever with us.

—*Middleton*

The commandment is a lamp; and the law is light; and reproofs of instruction are the way of life.

—*Proverbs*

To have striven, to have made an effort, to have been true to certain ideals — this alone is worth the struggle.

—*William Osler*


The behavior of men to the lower animals and their behavior to each other bear a constant relationship.

—*Herbert Spencer*


They shall march every one on his ways . . . Neither shall one thrust another; they shall walk every one on his path.

—*Joel*


The "squeaky wheel" is self imposed friction and self destruction.

—*A Fact*


The means are always greater than the ends.

—*Mahatma Gandhi*


Let us have faith that right makes might, and in that faith let us to the end dare to do our duty as we understand it . . . I know I am right because I know that liberty is right, for Christ teaches it.

—*Abraham Lincoln*

We cannot do without God; and of Him we are sure. All that science and criticism can urge cannot shake the self evident truth that He asks me to be true, just, merciful and loving, and because He asks me to be so, I know that He is Himself what He requires of me.

—*John Greenleaf Whittier*

Christianity is the good man's text; his life, the illustration.

—*J. P. Thompson*

We must each chop our own wood and let the chips fall where they may.

—*JML*

Stand porter at the door of thought.

—*Mary Baker Eddy*

Nothing will ever be attempted if all possible objections must be first overcome.

—*Samuel Johnson*

Thought takes man out of servitude into freedom.

—*Emerson*

The first rule of education, in all lands, is never to say anything offensive to anyone.

—*Voltaire*

Do well the little things now; so shall great things come to thee by and by asking to be done.

*—Persian Proverb*

From the lowest depth there is a path to the loftiest height.

*—Carlyle*

Peace comes to him who brings it; Joy to him who gives it; but perfect understanding only to him who loves perfectly.

*—Elbert Hubbard*

Youth is not a time of life; it is a state of mind.

*—Robert Frothingham*

From now guard your thoughts; for it is true that yesterday's wrong thought gives birth to the trials of today; it is equally certain that today's right thinking will generate joy for the morrow.

*—Hope La Gallienne*

Be forgetful of favor given; be mindful of blessings received.

*—Chinese Proverb*

Anger blows out the lamp of the mind.

*—Robert Ingersoll*

There is one thing stronger than armies: an idea whose time has come.

*—Victor Hugo*

God gives you His spiritual ideas, and in turn, they give **you** daily supplies.

—*Mary Baker Eddy*

The most acceptable service to God is doing good to man.

—*Benjamin Franklin*

Behavior is a mirror in which everyone displays his image.

—*Goethe*

Be a brother to the children of thy Father.

—*Sotah*

The jealous man poisons his own banquet and then eats it.

—*Anon.*

He enjoys true leisure who has time to improve his soul's estate.

—*Thoreau*

How rare the soul quiet enough to hear God speak.

—*Anon.*

It is with words as with sun rays: the more they are condensed the deeper they burn.

—*Southey*

Only by being nearer to God than I am could anything separate me from God.

—*JML*

Our thoughts beget our actions; they make us what we are.

—*Mary Baker Eddy*